THE TIMELESS DOMINIC
A COMMENTARY ON THE *O LUMEN*

THE TIMELESS DOMINIC

A COMMENTARY ON THE *O LUMEN*

Richard T.A. Murphy, O.P.

With an Introduction by
William R. Bonniwell, O.P.

CLUNY MEDIA

Cluny Media edition, 2015

This Cluny edition includes minor editorial revisions to the original text
including deletion of obsolete references.

Text of *The Timeless Dominic* copyright © Richard T.A. Murphy, O.P., 1967,
published by permission

Text of "Introduction" by William R. Bonniwell, O.P.
copyright © St. Cecilia Congregation

Cluny Media edition copyright © 2015 Cluny Media LLC

Photographs copyright © 2015 St. Cecilia Congregation,
LBP Communications, Inc.

ISBN: 9781944418168

Foreword by Sr. Matthew Marie Cummings, O.P.
Congregation of St. Cecilia, Nashville, TN

Photographs by Sister Mary Justin Haltom, O.P.
Images of the life of St. Dominic, Chapel of St. Cecilia,
Congregation of St. Cecilia, Nashville, TN

Cover design by Clarke & Clarke

Cover image: *St. Dominic*, Franz Meyer of Munich
Permission granted by Fr. Lawrence Lew, O.P.

Contents

Preface

Few people have the time, space or ability to praise St. Dominic, the founder of the Dominican Order, as he deserves. But as the Chinese proverb reminds us, it is better to light a single candle than to bewail the darkness.

If in his honor we cannot light a giant candle similar to those which burn at Lourdes or Fatima or other shrines, we feel that St. Dominic will, in his great fatherly charity, be satisfied—perhaps even somewhat amazed—at our tiny little taper. Slender as it is, we light it in the hope that it will burn brightly—well, bravely, at least—in his honor.

O LUMEN

O light of the Church, teacher of Truth, rose of patience, ivory of chastity. You freely poured forth the waters of wisdom. Preacher of grace, unite us with the blessed.

Timeline of the Life of St. Dominic

1170   Dominic de Guzman is born in Caleruega, Spain.

1184   Dominic attends the university in Palencia.

1190   Dominic is appointed a canon at Osma.

1203   Dominic accompanies his holy bishop to the Marches of France.

1206   On the feast of Saint Mary Magdalen, Saint Dominic has a vision.

1207   Bishop Diego dies and Saint Dominic takes charge of the small band of preachers.

1211   Saint Dominic's prayers save drowning pilgrims.

1215   Dominic goes to the Lateran Council.

1216   Pope Honorius III succeeds Innocent III. Dominic receives approval for the Order.

1220   The first General Chapter of the Order is held in Bologna around Pentecost, 1220.

1221   Death of St. Dominic—Friday, August 6, 1221.

1234   Canonization of St. Dominic.

Foreword

The republishing of *The Timeless Dominic*, written by Richard T. A. Murphy, O.P., during this 800th anniversary of the founding of the Dominican Order is indeed timely! In an era when we are constantly challenged to preach the gospel anew, *The Timeless Dominic* will increase our zeal to follow in the footsteps and the holiness of St. Dominic. Preachers on fire with the same mercy that filled the heart of Dominic are needed today no less than in the time when the Dominican Order was established.

St. Dominic is referred to in the *O Lumen* as Light, Doctor, Rose, Ivory, Dispenser, and Preacher. All of these titles are included in the plea invoking Dominic to unite us with the Blessed. Dominic's unfathomable love for God and neighbor directed his every thought, action, and prayer to the salvation of souls.

The *O Lumen* is not only an ancient hymn in praise of St. Dominic, but it is also a pattern of life formed by the gospel for all of us to live our calling faithfully, no matter the state of life.

May this commentary enrich us and stoke the flames of zeal in us, so that we may be zealous preachers of the truth, in the likeness of St. Dominic.

Sr. Matthew Marie Cummings, O.P.

They shall be called sons of God

Approbation of the Order of Preachers by Honorius III

Introduction

The exquisite rhythmic antiphon—*O lumen Ecclesiae*—was composed by Constantine, bishop of Orvieto. The inspiration which caused him to create this little gem was twofold: the profound holiness of St. Dominic and his remarkable service to the Church.

The author of this book, Father Richard T. A. Murphy, will set forth the holiness of the saint; it will be my privilege to describe the outstanding service Dominic rendered the Church.

Archbishop Alban Goodier, S.J., once wrote: "There is a chapter in the history of Europe which seems never yet to have been adequately written. It is the chapter which should record the debt owed by Europe and all Christendom to St. Dominic and his sons, the Order of Preachers, during a period of Europe's greatest crisis. At a time when every force, spiritual as well as political, threatened to tear

Christendom asunder...St. Dominic did more than any other man of his time to keep it one."

St. Dominic was born at Caleruega in Spain, in 1170 or 1171. As he was of noble birth, his elementary schooling was private. Then he was sent to the famous schools at Palencia, where he remained for ten years. For six years he studied the liberal arts, after which he devoted four years to studying theology and Scripture.

Ordained a priest, he became a Canon Regular of St. Augustine at Osma. In 1203, he accompanied his bishop, Diego, on a royal mission to Denmark. Two years later, he again went with Diego to Denmark, after which both men visited Rome, Citeaux, and finally Montpellier. It was here that they met the Cistercian abbots sent by Pope Innocent III to convert the Albigensians. As this meeting entirely changes Dominic's life, it is important for us to recall who these Albigensians were.

At the time the Church was facing one of its greatest crises—the struggle with the powerful Neo-Manichaean heresy. In the third century, Manichaeism had inflicted grave harm on the Church; in the eleventh century, there had been a rebirth of this error in Bulgaria and from here it spread over most of Europe.

The sect was split into some twenty variants, which are usually grouped together under the one convenient (but not quite accurate) name of Albigensian heresy. But all denied fundamental doctrines of Christianity—especially the divinity of Christ. They said that the Christ who died on the cross was wicked. They rejected most of the Bible as well as the seven sacraments. They claimed the human body is evil; hence, to destroy it by suicide is a good deed. Marriage is sinful and to have children is evil. These sectaries called themselves Christians, but there was little of Christianity in their doctrines.

One may wonder how, in the "Ages of Faith," such doctrines could take deep root in the very heart of Christendom. The reasons are so hard to believe that we quote only official Church documents—the acts of national synods, the decrees of ecumenical councils, and the letters of Pope Innocent III.

The first reason was the ignorance of the laity, many of whom knew little about their religion. Their ignorance was due to an ignorant clergy, who were the product of inferior theological schools. A rich diocese usually had a complete staff of competent professors, but a poor diocese could afford only one or two teachers for the whole curriculum. As poorer dioceses paid only starvation salaries, they usually got—Pope Innocent III remarked—just what they paid for. The haphazard and incompetent way many schools were run resulted in instances of men being ordained who could not read, much less write.

The National Synod of Oxford (1222) urged "that priests learn to read correctly *at least* the words of the Canon of the Mass." The Fourth Lateran Council (1215) ordered "that bishops who ordain ignorant men should be severely punished." Innocent III was obliged to remove from office some thirty bishops— some of whom knew nothing whatever of theology.

This almost incredible situation was aggravated by a more shocking evil.

While the majority of the clergy led blameless lives, there were many instances of concubinage. The acts of the Second and Third Lateran Councils denounce such priests, call for their removal and for the punishment of the bishops who tolerated such scandals. The infamous lives of a relatively small percentage of the clergy brought odium and contempt on all.

A third cause for the spread of heresy was the wealth of many prelates. Most bishops and abbots lived as luxuriously as temporal lords. Their appearances in public, accompanied by several hundred knights (who were in their pay) and a multitude of servants, caused much scandal. This display of wealth grew so excessive that the Third Lateran Council limited to thirty(!) the number of horsemen a bishop might take with him on a visitation of his diocese. Moreover, the Council insisted, the bishop was to leave at home his falcons and hunting dogs.

Many earnest Christians realized that these scandals were the reasons why so many defected from the Church; but they did not see how the problem could be solved. Some tried partial solutions, as did two priests—independently of each other—Robert d'Arbrissel (d. 1117) and Norbert of Xanten (d. 1134). Both these men distributed their wealth to the poor, and clad in coarse robes, went barefoot from village to village, preaching the gospel. Other reformers were laymen, like Peter Waldo, who also gave away his wealth and embracing poverty, preached the gospel throughout the city of Lyons. Not having any theological training, Peter and his followers soon fell into heresy.

Innocent III finally realized that something more than apostolic poverty and moral exhortations were needed. Only theologians could expose the errors of these sects and establish the truth of Christianity. So the Pope sent twelve Cistercian abbots to Languedoc¹ to be missionaries. The abbots labored there for some years but converts were few.

When the abbots preached on the holiness of the Church, their listeners derisively named the priests who were living in open concubinage; and their list always began with Berengar, the archbishop of Narbonne, who was notorious for his greed, immorality, and simony. Papal legates urged the Pope to punish this evil prelate, and alarmed at their action, Berengar went to Rome. All Languedoc watched the case. Then came the thunderbolt. Innocent III, ignoring the pleas of his legates, pardoned Berengar and restored him to his see.

The Albigensians hailed this as proof that the Church was rotten to the core, because the "Vicar of Christ" had in effect condoned the Archbishop's evil life. With this blunder, the Pope had ended all hope of converting the Albigensians. Later, he would remove Berengar from office; but it was too late, the harm had been done.

---

1. This area comprised a considerable part of southern France; it did not then have a name for the whole region. Later, it was called Languedoc, after the dialect spoken there.

Meanwhile, the Cistercian abbots in Languedoc were stunned. They assembled at Montpellier to decide whether it was worthwhile to continue their efforts. It was at this juncture (1206) that Bishop Diego and Dominic reached the city. They persuaded the abbots to persevere and volunteered to join them; but a year later Diego died and the abbots went home. Dominic was left with only a few others.

Undismayed, he determined to continue. The Albigensians insisted that not one could preach the gospel sincerely if he did not live as an apostle, that is, dress poorly, travel on foot, have no luggage, possess no money, and beg his daily bread; for this reason, people would not listen to any preacher who was not "poor." To gain a hearing, Dominic and his followers preserved the "apostolic poverty" they had adopted in 1206. They did this in a region that was not friendly but hostile; where priests were hated and often maltreated and where a number of priests had been murdered. When Dominic was refused lodging, he would calmly sleep at the side of the road, a tempting target for the dagger of a fanatical bigot.

It was while leading this dangerous life among the Albigensians that Dominic realized the need of a religious order especially trained for this kind of apostolate. He began to plan its formation. Of all the great Churchmen of the Middle Ages, he was the first—and for a long time the only one—to grasp the complete solution of a problem that had plagued the Church for centuries, the effective handling of doctrinal errors.

Meanwhile, he continued trying to win converts. His perseverance and his magnificent courage in the face of personal danger attracted other priests to him, and thus was born the Order of Preachers. But being poor and living by begging, the infant order for the next half-dozen years had no home. It was not until April, 1215, that a house in Toulouse was given to them and the friars were able to live together and "observe the practices of the religious life." Fulk, bishop of Toulouse, now canonically established them in his diocese.

But both Dominic and Fulk were aware that a permission granted by one bishop may be withdrawn by his successor. To ensure permanence to this project, the saint needed papal approval. Since the Bishop was leaving for Rome to attend the Lateran Council, he took Dominic with him. Together they had their audience with Innocent III. This was the first week of October—a whole month before the Council opened.

The saint had two requests to make. The first was to obtain papal protection for the convent of cloistered nuns he had established at Prouille in 1207. This petition was readily granted. But the second petition must have startled the Pontiff. Dominic wanted papal approval of something which had never been granted before: he wanted his order to be called an Order of Preachers, and that it be in reality an order of preachers.

He was not asking for permission merely to exhort the people to lead good lives; such permission had often been granted by the pope to groups of laymen—to the *Humiliati*, to the converts under

Durando of Huesca, to Bernard Prim and his band, to Francis of Assisi and the Friars Minor. Dominic insisted that his friars should be allowed to preach on dogmatic as well as moral subjects; that they be preachers in fact, not merely exhorters. Today, such a request would cause no surprise; in the thirteenth century it was revolutionary.

From the time of the apostles, the privilege of preaching was regarded as the prerogative of the bishop. The term *ordo praedicatorum* in patristic tradition meant only one body of men—the episcopate, the men who preach by reason of their office. When a pastor or some other person preached, he did so, not by reason of his priesthood, but because he had been delegated by his bishop. This was why Dominic's request was so startling: he wanted his priests to have the right to preach by reason of their membership in the Order.

Unprecedented as his plan was, he realized that anything less would be of little value. Without papal authorization to preach dogmatic sermons, the purpose of his organization would be defeated, for his friars would often be denied permission to preach by worldly bishops who would not want to be disturbed; by bishops of heretical leaning; by bishops suspicious of poorly-clad preachers, especially if these begged their bread. For begging was considered degrading for a priest; moreover, it was the very means used by Albigensian leaders to win the confidence of the people.

It is ironical that Innocent III, who tried so many ways to eradicate religious error, when offered a plan

that would succeed, failed to recognize his opportunity. Perhaps he thought Dominic's idea was too
revolutionary, too great a break with tradition; or
he feared it would arouse resentment among the
bishops who were then assembling for the Council.
Whatever his reason, he temporized by giving the
plan to a cardinal "for further examination."

One month later, on November 11, the Council opened. It showed little independence. The
Roman Curia had prepared seventy decrees. The
bishops passed all of them; they altered none,
they introduced none of their own. Since the
Curia does not send decrees to an ecumenical
council without the pope first having approved of
them, Innocent III had seen Canon 13 (forbidding
the institution of any new order) and indeed had
probably inspired it. He published the decrees of
the Council on December 14.

Shortly after his proclamation, Dominic had
his second audience with the Pope. The latter used
Canon 13 as his reason for not granting the saint his
request. He told Dominic to return to his compan-
ions at Toulouse, and after they had unanimously
chosen an already approved rule, to return for papal
approval.

The friars at Toulouse unanimously chose the
Rule of St. Augustine, the rule St. Dominic had lived
under since his ordination. This rule was sufficiently indeterminate that it would not interfere one iota
with the saint's plan. He returned to Rome to find
Innocent III had died and Honorius III had become
Pope. The latter approved the plan and issued a

bull to that effect on December 22, 1216. A new idea of a religious order had been launched.

Dominic now dispersed his friars to various cities, and within four years the Order had spread over continental Europe even to the borders of Russia. Perhaps Dominic now knew that his death was not far off;[2] in any case, it was time to complete the Dominican rule of life, so he notified the priories throughout Europe to send delegates to Bologna for a general chapter in 1220.

The meeting was not called merely for routine approval. The delegates were allowed to discuss, modify or reject their founder's suggestions. In granting this absolute freedom, Dominic was introducing a degree of democracy that was a novelty in religious orders. That this democracy was real is shown by the fact that the delegates did reject two of Dominic's proposals. One was to retain the extreme form of poverty that he and his first friars had practiced since 1206.[3] The capitulars feared that this might prove a hindrance to study; therefore, they modified it.

The delegates also rejected the suggestion that lay brothers have the care of all temporal matters—as had been the custom in the Order of Grandmont for over a century; this would give the fathers more time for study. But the capitulars thought that such a plan was too liable to abuse, so the proposal was defeated.

---

2.   He died August 6, 1221.

3.   This shows the error of those who claim Dominic borrowed the idea of poverty from the Franciscans. In 1206, there was no Franciscan Order, and it would be several more years before Francis would be converted.

Despite these two setbacks, Dominic won approval for what has proved to be one of the finest constitutions in the whole Church; one that would efficiently guide the Order for centuries to come. There would never be the need of a second or of a third rule. The clarity and completeness of the constitution would save his friars from furious quarrels concerning its interpretation; its farseeing provisions would safeguard the Order from the divisions which split other orders of the Church; and its many perfections would be copied by other orders for centuries to come.

Today, all orders of priests preach dogmatic as well as moral sermons; but Dominic was the first to obtain approval from the Church for so novel an idea. Today, priests of all orders must study ecclesiastical sciences; but Dominic was the first to formally dedicate his order to such study. Today, all great orders have one international head; but Dominic was the first to achieve such unity. Today, most orders elect their superiors; but it was Dominic who introduced a genuinely democratic way of doing this. He was also the first founder to exempt his priests from manual labor; they were to use their time only for study, prayer, and preaching. Until Dominic's day, only illness or physical impossibility excused from the obligation of the rule; Dominic was the first to insist that dispensations from the rule were to be granted whenever the salvation of souls would benefit thereby.

Not everything in the Dominican constitutions was original. When the saint saw in another rule something that was ideal for his purpose, he did not hesitate to adopt it. He selected some customs from the Benedictines, and chose many things from Citeaux and Prémontré. It was probably from the Knights Templar or from the Hospitallers of St. John that he took the idea of a centralized order under one head. But whatever he borrowed, he adapted to form a harmonious and perfectly coordinated system of government.

There is another noteworthy facet to this jewel of legislation—its adaptability. The contrast between life in the thirteenth century and that of the twentieth and twenty-first centuries is extreme. One was a slow, leisurely way of life which began with sunrise and ended shortly after sunset; the other is a busy, crowded schedule which often turns night into day. Many of the problems of that remote era are gone, but a host of new ones has taken their place. Yet the Dominican constitutions function as efficiently in the present century as they did eight hundred years ago. Such wonderful flexibility is another proof of the vision and genius of St. Dominic.

It is not strange that critical historians, Catholic and Protestant alike, have heaped praise on this great document. They declare: "It is perfectly devised"; "It is truly remarkable for its age"; "It is the work of a constructive statesman." The Lutheran historian, Albert Hauch, asserts: "It is the most perfect of all the monastic organizations of the Middle Ages."

St. Dominic's superb gift to the Church—*The Constitutions of the Order of the Friars Preachers*—has well merited for the saint the apostrophe—*O lumen Ecclesiae!* O Light of the Church!

Blessed Jane's Vision

I

Light of the Church

Saints have a way of accumulating titles which summarize and describe their life's work. Some are called patrons of the poor, of the missions, of travelers, soldiers and sailors, of students, even of alcoholics. Others have acquired such titles as Friend of the Orphan, Protector of the Poor, and so on. St. Dominic is saluted in the *O Lumen*, a hymn which his sons and daughters sing daily in his honor, as *Light of the Church*.

It is intriguing that the first thing Constantine de Medici,[1] the author of the *O Lumen*, associated with St. Dominic was light, beautiful, intangible, mysterious light.

---

1. Constantine of Medici entered the Order shortly after Dominic's death and, ca. 1254, became Bishop of Orvieto. He is the author of the *Legenda B. Dominici primi fundatoris Ordinis Fratrum Praedicatorum*, otherwise known as the *Legenda nova*, and of the Office to be said on St. Dominic's feast. Constantine died in 1258 (Quetif-Echard, *Scriptores O.P.*, (Paris; 1719), I 153f.).

LIGHT

The word light was frequently found on our Lord's lips. He used it in describing what was to happen on Judgment Day: some were to be cast forth into darkness where there would be weeping and gnashing of teeth, but the others would sit down with him at the joyful, lightsome, messianic banquet. Jesus is descried in the Fourth Gospel as *the true light which was coming into the world and enlightening all men.* He called his disciples *the light of the world.* Light and shadow play constantly about Christ, the Way, the Truth, and the Life.

Light and mystery, now there's a strange paradox. The blind cannot imagine what light is except in terms of the other senses (soft, warm, cold, and the like). But those born with sight likewise find it difficult to describe. The most articulate scientist gropes for words when he talks about light, and in the end he too must speak, inadequately, of light waves or particles or subatomic atmospheres, none of which does justice to the glory that is light. Only artists find it a congenial medium of expression. One of the remarkable attractions of the Spanish Pavilion at the New York World's Fair was a picture by Salvador Dali, cryptically entitled *The Key of Life.* This painting shimmered and glowed with light, and, to some bedazzled viewers at least (myself included) seemed to pour out of the picture and fill the room with splendor.

There are lightsome *people.* Some have only to walk into a room, and it becomes at once a brighter and more cheerful place. St. Dominic's biographers and those who testified at his canonization are unanimous in recalling his sunny disposition. He seemed to walk in light; there was about him a kind of shining gaiety: his face shone, he was pleasant to everybody. Before his birth his mother dreamed she saw the whole world illumined by the flaming torch a dog held in its mouth, and she interpreted the dream as referring to the child she carried in her womb.[2] A psychiatrist might sniff at such a story, and the sophisticated find it hopelessly naïve, but it comes from a respectable source, and later events proved its accuracy. Dominic was a good watchdog of the Lord, arousing sinners to their peril by his barking, and by his teaching and preaching illuminating a good part of France, Spain, and Italy.

According to another story, Dominic's godmother saw a star on his forehead when he was being baptized.[3] A portent? Perhaps. In any case the star and the dog have become symbols of St. Dominic. He is the saint with the eight-pointed star. Artists, and Dominican heraldry, have borrowed these elements. It is light's function to reveal what lies shrouded in the darkness. Dominic's light does not emanate from his books, for the simple reason that he wrote none, but flows in great floods from his life. Blessed Cecilia attributed to him a "certain radiant splendor of countenance."

---

2.   See the comment on this in W. A. Hinnebusch, O.P., *The History of the Dominican Order* (Staten Island: Alba House, 1966), I, 16.

3.   Ibid.

As a young man at the University, Dominic first manifested his undeniable verve and color. When famine struck the university town, Dominic sold his valuable, personally annotated sheepskin manuscripts, and with the money bought food for the starving. "How can anyone study from dead skins," he asked, "while living men are dying of hunger?" This action, and the noble phrase that accompanied it, bring Dominic into focus as a man of compassion and mercy, but also as a man of almost military sharpness of judgment.

We know that a man's speech and his reading are a fair index of his character. We also know that Dominic liked to read the Gospel according to St. Matthew and the epistles of St. Paul, and that his thoughts and conversation revolved about God and his book, the Bible. If he were living today, Dominic would be a famous biblical theologian, known for his views on the meaning and purpose of life, the effects of Adam's sin, God's plan to rescue sinful man, divine mercy, love and justice, and, of course, man's abuse of God's gifts, not the least of which was heresy, the Albigensian heresy.

Now light is for sharing, not for hiding under a basket, and Dominic was more than eager to share his light. All who knew him knew also of his tremendous zeal, and to illustrate this there is a story about an encounter he had with an innkeeper. One might reasonably suppose, from the fact that Dominic was in an inn at all, that he had reached it footsore and weary after a long day on the road. But when he saw the chance to speak about God and his creature, man, he forgot his fatigue, and spent the night arguing with his host. It is recorded that as dawn's light crept into the sky, the light of grace came flooding into the innkeeper's soul.

Something like that dawn, in whose light men began to see their lives with God in the picture, seemed to occur regularly whenever Dominic began to speak on his favorite topic, God. Warm and outgoing, Dominic was like a luminous dial which, momentarily held to the light, glows for a long time afterwards with the light. Dominic's light was enkindled and nourished by his close union with God. He bequeathed to his order something of his own clarity of vision and intense zeal, and his sons and daughters have in their turn shed luster on the Church.

To call a man a *light* means, we should say today, that he is a man of unusual ability, outstanding, a star of exceptional brilliance. To be called a star is flattering, but ... it has its drawbacks. Perhaps one of the reasons why St. Dominic has never become a really popular saint lies in his association with mysterious, intangible, elusive light. It is a fact that Dominic is often referred to as an intellectual, which is more than enough to steer some people away from him; many feel ill at ease in the company of intellectuals. But Dominic has other assets beside brains; he is a saint. The Church assures us of this. Whether then he is accepted or neglected by many does not really matter. His own children are proud that their father is not only a bright star, but a genuine *Light of the Church.*

CHURCH

The word "church" is a term, both rich and complex, which is borrowed from the Old Testament *gahal* or *ecclesia*, the Hebrew and Greek words for the solemn "assembly" of the chosen people (see Deut 4:10; 9:10; 18:16). The term was at first used by the messianic community of the early Church and then, keeping pace with the rapid expansion of Christianity, acquired an ever-wider meaning: the mother church in Jerusalem (Acts 8:1), the churches of Judea (Gal 1:22), house churches (Rom 16:5), the Church of God (Acts 20:28), the body and the Spouse of Christ (Col 1:18; Eph 5:23ff.). Finally, the Church came to be seen in a cosmic perspective (Eph 1:22ff.).

Many associate *church* with the place where they made their First Holy Communion or attended Mass as children. But the Church is more than just a place. Some associate it with other activities found in almost every parish: card-parties, bazaars, picnics, and so on. But the Church is more than the giving of self, service, joy, and the laughter of friends. Some look upon the church as a place where priests talk money all the time (tithing, special collections, and the like). But the Church is not a financial institution. Neither is she a charitable organization with religious overtones, a welfare agency, or counseling bureau, supplementing or competing with federal projects to help delinquents, high school dropouts, unwed mothers, and so on. Many of these social services she does indeed supply, and in her own kind way, but she is more than just that. She is *a sign* and *an instrument of salvation, of union with God.*[4] She is God's presence in the world, and a perpetual memorial of the unity of the human race under God, the kingdom of God on earth.

The Scriptures tell us of God's incredible plan to elevate his creature, man, to share in his divine life. Even after all men had fallen in Adam, God offered them the means of salvation in view of Christ the Redeemer. He planned that "those who believe in Christ should be assembled in that holy Church which, already foreshadowed from the origin of the world, prepared for in a remarkable way in the history of the people of Israel and in the old covenant, and established in a new era of time, was manifested by the outpouring of the Spirit and which at the end of time will achieve its glorious consummation...."[5] "To carry out the will of the Father, Christ inaugurated the kingdom of heaven on earth, revealed to us the mystery of himself, and by his obedience effected our redemption. The Church, that is, the kingdom of Christ now present in mystery, grows visibly in the world through the power of God....All men are called to this union with Christ."[6] And even now, "the entire Church appears a people made one with the unity of the Father and the Son and the Holy Spirit."[7]

---

4.   Cf. Second Vatican Council's *Dogmatic Constitution on the Church* (*Lumen gentium*), n. 1.

5.   Ibid., n. 2.

6.   Ibid., n. 3.

7.   Ibid., n. 4.

It is not easy for men to speak of divine things, because our words are too limited to do them justice. We therefore multiply our words, and by this very multiplication, understand a bit more of the mystery of the Church.[8] The Church is a *sheep-fold* (Jn 10:1–10); Dominic spared no efforts to lead the Lord's sheep to it. She is *God's building* (1 Cor 3:9); Dominic helped raise and defend it. She is *God's field* (ibid.); Dominic cultivated it. She is *God's chosen vine* in his favorite *vineyard*; Dominic tended and pruned them so that they might bear more fruit. The Church is *built on the foundation which is Christ* (Mt 21:42 *loc. Par.*); Dominic drew his strength from her. She is the *house of God* (1 Tim 3:15), *God's dwelling place* with men (Rev 21:3), *his holy temple*, (Eph 2:19ff.); Dominic was a good and faithful steward. She is the *bride of Christ* (Rev 19:7; 21:2, 9: Eph 5:25); Dominic, the *friend of the bridegroom* (Jn 3:29), served Christ gladly, and on hearing his voice, rejoiced exceedingly in his presence. The Church is *God's presence in the world*; Dominic sought to make men see it as such. Men enter the Church by way of baptism, and are sanctified in it by the sacraments, especially by the Eucharist, the sacrament of unity.

The pilgrim community or churchly people of God is a visible structure governed by a hierarchy and the Holy Spirit, a complex reality which needs both human and divine guidance. And this societal Church which the Savior entrusted to Peter's keeping "subsists in the Catholic Church governed by Peter's

---

8.   The images which follow are treated in §6 of the *Constitution*.

successor and by the bishops in communion with him."[9] Many elements of holiness and truth are to be found outside the Church's visible structure, both among other Christians and non-Christians alike, for God is free to dispose of his gifts as he likes. However, outside the Church such gifts are *extraordinary* signs of God's will to save men; within the Church which Dominic served, they are normal and almost, one might say, the ordinary, assured possession of all the faithful. Outside, men "seek the unknown God in shadows and images,"[10] whereas within, man lays hold of the reality and already lives the life of glory, thanks to faith, and those means of salvation, the sacraments, which are found in the Church.

St. Dominic was a faithful son of this marvelous Church. A man of mystery, baptized in the faith, a stranger to sin and a priest of God, the trusted companion and adviser of bishops, he was a true apostle. So well did he carry out Christ's command to proclaim the truths of salvation, that he fully merits the splendid title, *Light of the Church*, given to him by Bishop Constantine of Orvieto.

---

9.   Ibid., nn. 4 and 8.

10.   Ibid., n. 16.

Dominic Studying Under the Tutelage of His Uncle

2

Doctor of Truth

It was observed after his death that President John F. Kennedy had been in the habit of doodling on the blotter of his White House desk. Many people doodle when they have a chance, but what gave the President's doodling a particular significance was the fact that it so often consisted of a single word. That word, which appeared all over his blotter, in various sizes and at all angles, was—*decision*. An important word. No day passes but that the President of the United States makes decisions effecting the lives of its citizens, and the lives of millions of others whose destiny is tied in, one way or another, with that of America's.

The President is not alone in the matter of decisions. Every mature person shares this privilege and responsibility. To refuse to make up one's mind, to fail to chart a course, or not to follow through on decisions once made, is to live on a less than human level.

VOCATION

Youth's decisions involving the choice of a life's vocation are especially important. A vocation is something each man must decide for himself. The choice can be a difficult and painful experience, because there are so many things to choose from, and because a wrong choice early in life may have disastrous, sometimes irreversible, consequences. But no one is excused from making the choice, for all of that.

Although a man can work out his salvation in any walk of life, not all vocations are on the same level. There is a finely calibrated scale by which man's various callings are measured. They are judged, as a rule, by the value of the materials with which they deal. Miners, for example, and lumberjacks, farmers and fishermen,[1] all perform important and necessary tasks, without which the nation would perish. But such rough and ready men are not high society. A higher place is accorded the men who reshape basic materials for society's consumption, the merchants and businessmen. But they in turn are outranked by members of the medical profession, whose concern is the health of the community, the human body, and sometimes man's

---

1.   All these are skilled with their hands, each one an expert at his own work; Without them no city could be lived in, and wherever they stay, they do not go hungry. But they are not sought out for the council of the people, nor are they prominent in the assembly. They do not sit on the judge's bench, nor can they understand law and justice. They cannot expound discipline or judgment, nor are they found among the rulers. Yet they maintain the fabric of the world, and their concern is for exercise of their skill (Sir 38:31ff.)

psyche as well. As the object of their attentions is so important, doctors constitute what we usually call "society." They have both prestige and class.[2]

Keeping pace with doctors in importance are the teachers who make man's intellectual betterment their business.[3] Doctors prescribe medicine to relieve pain and cure sickness; teachers do something similar by dispensing truth, the only medicine which will cure the sickness of ignorance. It is a terrible sickness. How uncomfortable one can be when not "in the know," everyone knows. A young man who has not learned how to meet and talk to people is embarrassed when he finds he must hold up one end of a conversation. A girl who does not know how to dance (there are some!) or who is all feet when she tries to, finds that her lack of knowledge excludes her from a pleasant community pastime. How sad when heads of families sometimes have only their physical strength, their muscle, to exchange for bread for their families.

Ignorance of truth or lack of education makes life intolerable and dangerous, and society, recognizing this, encourages systems of public and private education. Those who reach the pinnacle of the teaching profession are rewarded with the coveted title of *Doctor*.

The science of medicine is valuable, and teaching is an honorable profession. But how shall we

---

2.   In Sirach 38, the medical profession is the first mentioned of those worthy of praise. "Make friends with the doctor for he is essential to you; God has also established him in his profession" (v. 1).

3.   Ibid., 39: 1–11 praises teachers.

sufficiently praise that profession which combines the good points of both teachers and doctors?[4]

The profession which deals not only with man's health and education, but with his eternal destiny as well, is beyond question one of the very highest. The world is a dark place for those who know nothing about its Lord and Creator, or about God's loving plan for man's salvation. When ignorance spills over into areas where justice and morality should prevail, anarchy is most likely to result. To cope with "spiritual illness, or ignorance" then there must be those who teach in and out of season the important lessons of right and wrong, of good and evil, sin and grace, heaven and hell. St. Dominic fits into this picture perfectly. These were the truths he dispensed to his contemporaries.

Society needs good teachers, good doctors, and good priests who will teach succeeding generations the truth about God, about man, and this world.

TRUTH

When a child is born he enters the world with a mind that is perfectly blank and unused. The ancient Romans compared it to a clean slate, a *tabula rasa*. But the slate begins to be used at once, because from the first moment of birth the senses (sight, smell, taste, hearing, touch) begin to operate. Smooth, automatic, and perfectly natural in their

4.   The priest is given the highest praise. Cf. the magnificent encomium of the high priest Simon, "glory of his people" (ibid, 50:1-11).

functioning, they begin to assemble that store of materials, of sensations, and so on, which are the raw material for thought. As we know, thought does not begin until the child reaches a certain age, but the child is always learning. He can depend on his senses to write on the slate.

But no man is wholly self-sufficient. A self-educated man may be a mine of information on his pet topic or topics, but oftener than not he will be quite at sea when it comes to the broader, overall view. Do-it-yourself learning is slow and difficult, and makes many mistakes which could have been avoided with the help of a teacher. Learning is usually much better if there is a good teacher at hand to provide the learner with balance and perspective.

Now a child's senses reach out for knowledge instinctively. Once a man reaches the age of reason, he begins to assimilate a higher kind of knowledge. And this is also in accord with his nature. Man's desire for truth is a hunger and a thirst, and in the course of history many people have died for the truth. During his trial, Jesus told his Roman judge, "I came into this world to bear testimony to the truth." Pilate, with an impatient "What is truth?"[5] turned away. He was not the first, nor yet the last, to behave thus in Truth's presence, and many share his conviction that truth is either unattainable, or something not worth the effort.

Now truth has many faces, all of them beautiful.

There is first of all the truth that is in things. A rose is a rose is a rose...a man is a man.... When in

5.   Jn 18:38.

his infinite power and wisdom God summoned the world into being, he was not all thumbs; he did not need practice to be perfect. What he created came into being exactly as he had intended it; there were no faulty models. All corresponded instantly and exactly to what he had in mind.

This kind of truth has a formidable name; it is called metaphysical or ontological truth. Forget the name; people who have never heard these names know what truth means. The politician laboring over his speech, the doctor setting a bone, the young girl setting her hair in a particular way, the housewife in a supermarket, all take this kind of truth, the truth that is in things, for granted. In their minds they have a picture; what they seek is the reality that corresponds to it.

There is also a kind of truth that is in the thinker, and it is called logical truth. When we speak to others, using their right names, we are functioning in terms of *logical* truth, that is, our minds have properly adjusted to facts outside of them, and properly assessed them. Who does not know the embarrassment of having called this person X, when he is in reality Y? In cases of mistaken identity, and error, our minds have not correctly wrapped themselves about extra mental reality, and the truth is not in them. Other people are who they are; when we recognize things as they are, we know the truth.

Of even greater practical importance is a third type of truth which we may call moral truth. It is called truth by courtesy only, but it is real for all of that. When a man's life matches what he believes,

when he puts his beliefs and convictions into practice, then, as the Bible says, he will "put on the truth,"
he will "walk in truth," and will "do the truth."

DOMINIC AND TRUTH

As a young man, Dominic was athirst for truth.
Did he not seek it at the best schools, at the University of Palencia? We know that he had a high appre-
ciation of education, but he did not hesitate to put it
off temporarily when he saw his neighbor in need.
Education is a means to an end, however, and he
pursued it relentlessly, and the Order's intellectual
orientation is certainly traceable to him. When he
established the Order, there were only twenty-five
doctors of theology in all Europe; fifty years later,
there were more than seven hundred, and many of
these were his followers.

Philip Hughes, the English historian, was once
asked what he considered the Church's greatest
danger, or the worst trail the Church had ever suf-
fered, and without a moment's hesitation, he an-
swered, "An ignorant clergy!"

With *truth* emblazoned upon its shield, Dominic's order has served the Church well. Dominican theologians and saints have sought out truth
in all its phases: they have taken up what God has
made, fitted their minds to it, and lived according
to their beliefs. They were not wells or cisterns but
ever-flowing springs which have kept the fields
of the Church constantly green. The Order was
hardly born when Dominic scattered the brethren

over the face of Europe, sending them to university centers. He silenced his critics with the remark, "Store grain in a barn and it will rot; sow it in a field, and you will reap a harvest." He was right. Truth is for the sowing, for the harvest, for use. As Shakespeare said:

> If our virtues did not go forth from us, 'twere alike
> as if we had them not.[6]

Some scholars look upon truth as a lifeless conforming of the mind to conclusions and statements formulated ages ago by scholars now long dead. Truth is anything but that. It is ever new, ever attainable. It is not a collection of timeless propositions; it is our way of keeping in touch with reality, and above all with that reality who said, "I am the Way, the Truth, and the Life" (Jn 14:6). Dominic's children are interested not only in the true and the false, as in mathematics, but in the truth which demands integrity and goodness of the part of the knower. Even the great Aquinas taught that, all things being considered, it would be better in this life—if one had to make such a choice—to be good than to be smart.[7]

Far from being the study of the dead past, then, truth is the study of all things that are. Like the Church, truth is living and apostolic. The Church's life pulsates strongly at the present moment, as a glance through any of our respectable magazines

---

6.   *Measure for Measure*, Act I, Scene I.

7.   *Summa Theologiae*, II a, IIae, q. 23, a. 6. ad I.

will show. It is, alas, true that the gleaners of truth are few, and that the harvest of truth is great. But quality counts for much. A few select scholars can, through their writings, help untold numbers of men and women draw closer to God in love.

The fact that Dominicans live in priories, parishes, and houses of study should never mean that they are sealed off from the world they serve. They keep alive to what is going on, and are ready to speak out when called upon. And even when not called up, they speak in their writings. There are problems enough to go around: Catholic life, the layman's role in the Church, parochial schools and the question of governmental aid, the expanding population, respect for life from conception to natural death, and marriage. The conciliar documents, especially the *Dogmatic Constitution on the Church* and the *Constitution on the Sacred Liturgy* must be familiar to us who serve the Church.

It seems to many that the situation introduced by the *aggiornamento* resembles nothing so much as the *tohu wabohu*, or chaos, of Genesis. But Genesis also noted that the Spirit was brooding over the face of this chaos, and that out of that brooding there came forth the wonderful universe in which we live.

There is darkness all about us, too, but we have a good guide in Dominic de Guzman, *Doctor of Truth*. He receives his light from the Church, and passes it on to us. Willing and eager to learn God's will, we grope with him towards the fulfillment of our mysterious destiny as an old order in a Church that is ever renewing herself. By conforming our lives to our faith, we shall prove ourselves to be worthy members of the Order of Truth.

> Beauty, goodness, and knowledge are three sisters
> That doat upon each other, friend to man,
> Living together under the same roof,
> And can never be sundered without tears.
>
> (Alfred Tennyson)

Dominic at Prayer Before the Crucifix

3

Rose of Patience

Life teaches us, and so does the Bible, that there is a time for everything. The seasons, the growth of the child in the womb, growing up, all take time. Nothing can be hurried. There is only one hour when it is right for an event to take place. So it was with Christ and his hour; it is ever so for all of us. We cannot hasten our hour, but we can learn to wait. It is not necessarily a time of inactivity, but it is definitely a time for waiting. Parents find that they must reassure their little ones, time and time again, that they will have to wait. There is a time for everything.

Back of this impatience, of course, is our chronic unhappiness over the delay of a desired good. For us, to see and to want are all one and the same; we dislike being put off, and if we had our way, we would have everything we wanted the instant we want it. God who is all patient must sometimes think we are peevish and petulant children. And short-sighted ones also. Always to be looking for what we have not, means that we are neglecting the golden opportunity offered us by the present moment. If the future is allowed to become everything, and if the present moment is treated with studied neglect, then the lovely virtues of perseverance and constancy, upon which so much of our natural and interior life depend, become irrelevant. When that stage is reached, we become poor indeed.

Behind our impatience is a gross misconception of the role *time* plays in God's plans. Hothouses provide us with exotic fruits in midwinter, but life (and God's plan) is not a hothouse. For each period there is an appropriate activity, and one has to learn to bide his time until the right moment arrives. We simply must learn to be patient.

A child can learn much from seeing his father "carry on" under trying circumstances, amid difficulties, under misfortune and good fortune. We are fortunate to have so patient a father. We do not salute him as a shy violet, because as a priest Dominic was a social man, always in the public eye, a man for all seasons, a servant of the Church. His name is not linked with the lily, traditionally reserved to the Blessed Mother and to St. Joseph. Dominic is, instead, compared to a rose, and is called a *rose of patience*. Many men would strenuously object to being compared to a flower, at least to some kinds of flowers. But the comparison with a rose is an excellent one. To be called a rose of patience means that Dominic is a beautiful example and model of patience.

On the ashtray I once acquired in Italy there ran the charming legend: *La rosa ha chi osa*, or "He who dares, obtains the rose!" The rose is defended by sharp thorns, and only one who is willing to risk shedding blood for it, gains it for himself. The title *Rose of Patience* links together two interesting ideas: the beauty of Dominic's patience, and the necessity and fact of his courage.

In the popular mind, virtuous action is often linked with weakness and effeminacy, rather than with beauty and strength. But the popular mind has often been wrong, and it is wrong here. Every true virtue calls for strength and skill. The word virtue signifies something *manly* and strong (cf. the Latin: *virtus*); it also implies that reason is in command, for a virtue is a consistent way of doing something smoothly and easily, and in a way that will redound to the doer's credit.

Professional musicians, athletes, dancers, and actors have acquired a consistency in skillful performance, and the attention and applause we give them is the tribute we pay to those who habitually do things well and honorable. In order to cope with the many varieties of human experience, men have to acquire many kinds of virtues. Some, like walking and dancing, are limited to the physical order; others are intellectual, like art and prudence; still others pertain to the moral order. The aim of the moral virtues (prudence, justice, courage, and temperance) is to attain to a way of acting that strikes the happy medium between too much and too little. There are also the theological virtues of faith, hope, and charity, but we are not going to treat of them here.

Patience belongs to the category of moral virtues, and is in fact a part of the virtue of courage. Talking about patience will not of course make anybody patient, but it may help put it in the best possible light. This noble virtue has gotten a bad press. One caricature of it is a man who is a doormat, or a punching bag; no one wants to be like that. Patience seems to indicate apathy and insensibility; few can be very stoical. In his *David Copperfield*, Dickens presents a savage parody on patience and humility, but few readers fail to spot the phony virtue and the hypocrisy of Uriah Heep.

There is, of course, genuine gold as well as imitation gold, true patience as well as shoddy imitations. It is a tribute to virtue that vice should try to imitate it. Vice dares not reveal its true face to the world, but hides its ugliness under a mask of goodness. It is regrettable that a beautiful virtue like patience should suffer neglect because it has been so often misunderstood.

Patience helps a man endure evil without being unduly cast down; it helps a man cope with present sorrow, whatever its cause; it helps him regulate his disappointment and frustration, and hold them in check so that they do not paralyze his activities. In other words, it is the opposite of "crying one's eyes out."

Despite the TV commercials in which people are always happy and contented, man's life on earth is always a warfare, a journey harassed by sorrow. For

some, sorrow is a constant companion. It is sometimes caused by sickness, or by failure, whether in
business or social relations or studies or raising
a family. Those whose marriage has never been
blessed with children know a special kind of sorrow.
Not even in the religious life is one a stranger to
sorrow. Life is a valley of tears, courtesy of our father
Adam. The important thing is to learn patience, or
how to live with sorrow intelligently, virtuously.

"Sorrow has destroyed many," as Ben Sirach
shrewdly observed, "and there is not profit in it."
Indeed, sorrow is one of the devil's best weapons. It
can arise from an infinite variety of causes, because
there is an infinite variety in the people, places, and
things which may rub against our grain, and cast
our spirits down. Sorrow arises from the realization
that we are caught in a situation that displeases us. A
law may prevent us from doing what we like, or the
coffee may not be hot, or the potatoes are burned,
or someone makes a noise when we want peace and
quiet, or another's mannerisms may grate upon us.
There is no shortage of sorrows.

Patience is directed at the evil which causes us
sorrow. In a bothersome situation there are a number
of things a patient man may do. He may try falling on
his knees and praying, but that, while good in itself,
is not always the reasonable or practical thing to do.
Another alternative is attack, striking at the cause
of sorrow and destroying it. This is an exhilarating
and noisy procedure, but not often very satisfactory,
for one has to replace what gets broken, and may
even have to face a counterattack which will render

the second condition worse than the first. A third solution, one not always possible nor advisable, is flight. But flight is not very satisfying, and it bears a strong resemblance to cowardice; moreover, it solves nothing, because in the long run the chief source of our unhappiness is ourselves. In the end, the best solution of all is to fight the enemy from inside, by exercising the virtue of patience.

True patience never calls upon a man simply to grin and bear it. He must do what he can to alleviate a situation. If the messy condition of his car or his lawn or his cellar bothers him he will clean things up. If he is sorrowed by a leaky faucet, he fixes it; if a loose carpet annoys him, he will tack it in place. And so on. He does what he can about removing the causes of his discontent, and in so doing he is acting reasonably, that is, virtuously. Such action does not mean that a man is impatient.

But there are times when there is nothing to do but to endure, with good grace, an unhappy situation. That kind of waiting is not complete inactivity. A deferred good is not the greatest calamity. God is the God of patience, St. Paul tells us. The Blessed Mother bore her sweet burden patiently for nine months, during which time she was obliged to put up with many inconveniences of travel, misunderstanding, even persecution. For thirty years she had to bear the trials of poverty, and then disgrace, for she stood beneath her son's cross. Mary is a wonderful example of the patience that controls sorrow. At the foot of the cross she did not swoon or collapse. She was also, as anyone can see, a brave woman.

Our Lord displayed a marvelous patience throughout his life. His hour was long delayed; his disciples were slow and dull of comprehension; his enemies persisted in distorting the meaning of his words, or tried to ensnare and compromise him. The scourging at the pillar, the way of the cross, the nails in his hands and feet, were evils which our Lord endured with patience. If he had not, the gracious act of man's redemption would never have taken place.

St. Dominic is an example of patience closer to home. A buoyant man, filled with plans for God's honor and glory, he frequently had to endure sorrow and frustration. As the traveling companion of Bishop Diego, he saw in France the evils that followed in the wake of the Albigensian heresy. But instead of just wringing his hands, he did his best to remedy the situation, putting in seven years at Fanjeaux, a tiny town in southern France, preaching the true gospel. And for seven years he met with failure. During those years his life was threatened, and he took a prudent precaution—he learned to bake his own bread, lest he be poisoned by the people of that village. On another occasion, at Caracassone, he asked a heretic for directions, and was deliberately led, barefooted friar though he was, through brambles and thorns till he was far from his desired destination. Even then his cheerfulness did not falter, because he was patient. Love has to be, first of all, patient (1 Cor 13:4).

Patience, which is for everybody, may not be the greatest of virtues (the love of God holds first place) but it accompanies all the virtues. Mary's patience was rewarded by the Christ child, and after that by her assumption and crowning in heaven. Dominic's patience was rewarded by a bountiful harvest of souls, and by the establishment of an order which has served the Church and mankind since the year 1216.

Blessed are those who are patient, for they too shall be rewarded. The reward consists, in part at least, in the acquisition of a wider perspective which takes the edge off the sorrows each day brings. Patience is for each day. No one wakes up to find himself finally perfectly resigned and patient; each day he has to resist that day's sorrow. Nor does the practice of patience become easier with age; older people are very often irritable and complaining, and need to practice patience.

In the convent of San Marco, in Florence, Fra Angelico has painted a marvelous fresco of St. Dominic, at the foot of the cross, looking up at Christ. Dominic's children must also keep their gaze directed at their suffering Savior when confronted with sorrow, and then they will not be depressed or discouraged, but will accept the pain and frustration as penance for their sins, and as a chance to prove their love for God.

The God of Christians is a God of patience (Rom 15:5). Jesus Christ, the divine Son of God, was a supreme model of patience. St. Dominic, chosen by God to be the founder of an order, also illustrates the beauty and strength of patience. He is rightly called *Rose of Patience*.

Blessed are the pure of heart

Dominic and His Children Under Mary's Mantle

4

Ivory of Chastity

F ew of the evils that dog man's footsteps fill
him with such terror and apprehension as the
prospect of going blind. Physical blindness is
on the whole, rather rare; of more frequent occur-
rence is a blindness that is self-inflicted, a blindness
of the spirit, a sort of selective vision whereby one
sees only what is wrong in other people, places, or
things. Some people can go out of doors on a beautiful June night and never see the stars, but only
how dark it is. This all-too-common blindness has
to be perseveringly resisted lest the good things
with which God has filled the world pass by us
unheeded and unappreciated. And a great pity that
would be, for to the reflective person all things can
awaken thoughts of God.

St. Dominic is saluted as the ivory of chastity.

IVORY

In ancient times, ivory was a rare, costly import from far-off Africa or India, and one is not surprised to find it in the ruins of the palaces of kings. Archaeological excavations conducted in Palestine and Egypt have brought to light many ivory fan handles, cane-handles, combs, elegant figurines (little statues), inlaid mirrors, even an inlaid bedstead!

Today one seldom hears of ivory except in reference to people who live in ivory towers (not intended to be complimentary) or who have heads of ivory (very unflattering). Much is said about our new alloys, about the woods and metals which have replaced ivory. But metals rust, alloys tarnish, and wood rots. Ivory grows more beautiful with age.

On my desk lies a letter opener made of ivory and exquisitely carved into the shape of a Chinese dragon. His back and tail are jagged and scaly, but his sides are smooth, and the overall picture is one of delicacy and beauty. Joannes, as I call him for a personal reason, is my pride and joy. Besides being decorative, he is surprisingly durable. He has opened many a letter for me, yet he is as sharp as ever, and the artistry of his persevering snarl holds me his appreciative captive.

Here then is one of ivory's greatest assets—its constancy or consistency, its ability to retain its shape. This ability to come into contact with harsh reality without being thereby changed or destroyed is what makes ivory the perfect symbol for loyalty and fidelity.

When men began to reconstruct Dominic's life they were struck by the fact that he enjoyed the company of women, especially of young women, and did so without ever sinning. Observers began to perceive how fine and noble and true a life he had led, and in the end expressed their admiration by calling him an *Ivory of Chastity*.

The combination of ivory and chastity requires a bit of explaining. If ivory belongs pretty much to the past, many today are of the opinion that chastity belongs there also. Many view with suspicion anyone who vows a life of chastity, which they interpret as hypocritical, impossible, selfish, or (especially) neurotic. That many favor and act upon a negative view of chastity can easily be deduced from the depressing statistics about venereal disease among high school students. Nor are the statistics concerning the sharp increase in the number of unwed mothers at all reassuring. Chastity is simply not popular today.

CHASTITY

Chastity is not a running away from people, an insensitivity to love or to other human beings; it is rather a special loving way of giving oneself to God and to man, an unswerving gift of one's whole self. Far from indicating a desiccation of the spirit or isolation from humanity, it is the way of life freely chosen by one who is willing to forget himself and is eager to give himself to others. Most men and women have a full human life in the married state; those who vow chastity commit themselves fully to the love of God and of other human beings in the single state. It is of this generous gift of self that ivory is the beautiful symbol.

The sexual instinct has been implanted in our natures by an all-wise God. Lying dormant during childhood, it comes clamorously to life in the teens. Powerful and imperious, sex is part of God's plan for the continuation of the human race. To this instinct he has joined the highest physical pleasure possible, and its enjoyment is part of the reward given to those who raise a family. That task occupies half a lifetime and is marked by many trials and heartaches; it is lightened by the spiritual love married partners feel for each other, and which finds expression in their mutual sharing of bodies.

Psychology and psychiatry have in recent years become familiar words to the common man. Beginning with Freud, attention has been called to man's deep emotions, to his inner drives and forces. If such emotions are repressed or unreasonably held in, he said, serious psychological disorders can result. It would be ridiculous to deny the existence of powerful forces within man. As Shakespeare once said, and truly,

> The strongest oaths are straw
> to the fire in the blood.[1]

But fire can be controlled and made to serve useful purposes. Some have stressed Freud's conclusion to justify indulgence in sexual matters, but the conclusion is by no means beyond challenge; ordinarily the control of the passions improves a man.

1.　*The Tempest*, Act 4, Scene 2.

Only the noblest of motives, then, should prompt the renunciation of the normal use of God-given instincts. Chastity as a way of life is, given the proper circumstances and reasons, an honorable and a good way of life. And it is possible to lead a chaste life. When a man or woman promises to serve God and neighbor while practicing chastity, God does not deny his graces to them, but more than matches their generosity.

In religious life the world over, young men and women each year deliberately and knowingly dedicate their lives to God, promising to serve him, and the world, while vowed to chastity. The world never ceases to be astonished at such a spectacle! It reveals man's capacity to be fully human, for it shows that man is after all only half an animal, and that the spirit of man, wherein he most resembles God, can command and control the lower part of his nature. Those who vow their chastity to God symbolize a love that is undivided, a dedication to God that is complete, and a disengagement from everything that is not God. Chastity is a mysterious sign to the world, recalling to it the chaste union which exists between Christ and the Church.

Why talk about chastity to those who have chosen it? It is a good thing, occasionally, to unwrap one's treasures and examine them more closely. People do this with jewels, and misers with money; why should we not admire the precious jewel of chastity? Life is not always a last-ditch struggle for control over the passions; there are times to enjoy the beauty of chastity.

The occasional re-evaluation of chastity serves to reassure those who have chosen it that they have done a good thing, and will help dispel any vain regrets which might be seeking entry in their thoughts. It is comforting to know that many of God's children have successfully asked this difficult path while serving God and the Church with distinction. Why should this be surprising? Chastity is a kind of love, and like all true love holds nothing back in the service of the beloved.

Another reason for talking about chastity is that it allows us to say once again that the body is not evil, that marriage is not something sinful or a lesser good. Virginity and chastity are virtues; marriage is a sacrament. The life of the spirit is more perfect than the life of the flesh, but St. Paul could think of nothing that so perfectly described the union of Christ and his Church as marriage. Plato, paganism's great thinker, taught that the body held the soul captive and prevented it from soaring upwards. This is not the Christian view at all. Not only is marriage a great sacrament, but, as both the Church and the Scriptures teach, man's body is God's creation, God's temple, the precious companion to the soul both here and in eternity.

A fourth and the original reason for considering chastity is that St. Dominic is called an *Ivory of Chastity*. There is nothing grim or joyless about him; he was no sour introvert. He made friends easily, and kept them over the years. Among those we know there were: Bishop Diego, Cardinal Ugolino, the talented people he drew into his order; the nuns of Prouille, or Madrid, or San Sisto Vecchio; and many stalwart lay men and women. The fact that Dominicans take a vow of chastity should mean that they are friendly, warm, and sympathetic, like St. Dominic. A mother sometimes says to her child, "Your father was a handsome man," and while the child may not know what handsome means, he suspects that it must be something good, and is proud of his father. And then he will try to model his life after that of his father.

The children of St. Dominic know that their father, the very *ivory of chastity*, was a handsome man. They will strive to imitate him in his unswerving gift of himself, in his constancy, in his charity, and above all in his warmth and friendliness to all.

They shall obtain mercy

Dispersal of the Brethren

5

Dispenser of
Wisdom's Waters

T he shining star on St. Dominic's forehead
calls to mind a constellation named Aquar-
ius, or Water Pourer, which appears in the
heavens, quite appropriately, during the rainy season
of the year. Young children, confined indoors by
the weather, have been known to chant plaintively,
"Rain, rain, go away, come again some other day." But
grown-ups know the importance of rain.

WATER

I remember standing one day atop the great
pyramid of Cheops, just outside of Cairo, Egypt.
The climb was well worth the effort, the view was
magnificent. The silent Sphinx kept its gaze fixed
eastwards, but my eyes were drawn to the south
and to the north, where flowed the majestic Nile,
flanked by wide fields of intense green. In ancient

days Egypt was the breadbasket of the East. More modern methods of irrigation have widened the fertile areas near the great river. But—and this sight caught me almost as an unexpected blow in the face—where the land is untouched by the life-giving waters of Mother Nile, the green instantly disappears. It is almost as if someone had trimmed the far edges of the fields with a giant scissors. On either side of the river, there is the green; beyond the green, looking hungrily into the gardens, is the desert, full of menace.

Far to the north, across the Mediterranean, the imposing remains of ancient Roman aqueducts rise into a lovely Italian sky. At the height of Rome's glory, fourteen of these aqueducts, three hundred miles underground, fifty-five above, brought water to imperial Rome. Each aqueduct bore a name: Virgo, Marcia, Claudia, and so on. The waters they carried varied in quality, the best of them being, of course, reserved for drinking. But none of the water was wasted. Large quantities of it, hot and cold, were required in the baths, and Rome's thirsty gardens had to be supplied too. Some of the water was diverted to the fountains which were (and are) scattered over the city, each with its own peculiar legend or history. What visitor has not thrown a coin into the famous fountain of Trevi, to insure a return trip to Rome before he dies! The Tortoise fountain adds beauty to a lower-class section of Rome, and atop the galloping horses in the Piazza Esedra, naiads disport themselves charmingly in jets of rushing water. Amusing, and a monument to man's irrepressible spirit, is Bernini's fountain in the Piazza Navona, perpetuating that artist's scorn for the façade of the adjacent Church which one of the popes, fearing too much Bernini in Rome, had given to a rival artist. And then there is nearby Tivoli, with its Ville d'Este, and its unforgettable variety of fountains.

The troubled spirit of man relaxes when he gazes upon the sea, whose waves mount upwards, move towards the shore, tumble over in grace, retreat in beauty, and then repeat their remarkable performance. Keats' beautiful Grecian urn was static; water, the friend of beauty and light, seems almost alive. A man does not have to take thought or even raise his finger, yet the tides rise and fall, rivers pursue their courses, and babbling brooks thread cheerful ways through the land. A thoughtful Creator has thus combined grace and beauty in this liquid thing so necessary for life.

Of all our resources, water is one of the most precious. Where it is available, civilization may flourish; when water disappears, vast cities, businesses, and cultures, are doomed. Today a man can walk dry-shod across the famous harbor of Ostia Antica, near Rome Ancient Ephesus, where Paul tarried for three years working and preaching the gospel, which now lies far inland. Because there is no discernible moisture on Mars or the moon,[1]

---

1. While scientists now know that liquid water does not exist on Mars or the moon, the current scientific consensus is that liquid water once existed on the Martian surface at some point in its history. Consequently, and without contradiction to the author's assertion, it is thus possible that simple life may have arisen on Mars and is currently an active focus of scientific inquiry.

scientists conclude life as we know it is non-existent there. Water is a prime necessity. It is no wonder then that we build reservoirs, regulate the flow of rivers by dams, and worry about the pollution of our streams. Without water, we should quickly perish.

WISDOM

St. Dominic was a dispenser of the waters of wisdom. "Where shall wisdom be found? Whence comes it?"[2] The question, "What is wisdom?" is one that has challenged great minds in every age, and we can learn from them something of the nature of wisdom and of St. Dominic.

There is more to human living than food and drink; "Man does not live by bread alone," as Christ once said. It has been remarked that once a man has taken care of the necessities of life, he begins to wonder and to ask questions. He is curious to know why there are different seasons, why the moon changes, the sun rises and sets, and the stars move so differently from the planets. What these and similar questions point to is the fact that man has an irresistible hankering for wisdom. It is a deeper and special kind of knowledge; not just many facts, not just quantitative knowledge, not mere speculation about things. Somewhere along the path of knowledge a mysterious alchemy takes place, transmuting knowledge into wisdom. Let us see if we can follow the process.

---

2.   Job 28:12, 20; Prov 8:11ff., Sir 24:1ff.

WISDOM AND KNOWLEDGE

Knowledge wears a number of faces with which we are all familiar. Her first face, known to every student, is science, mathematics, and physics. A second face is called theology. The third and last is a gift from on high which is called just that: the gift of wisdom.

First, then, science and math. Thanks to applied science, we live today amid comforts and conveniences undreamed of by our grandparents. This is quite all right with us; God made the earth and gave it to man to till, keep, subdue, and fill. In carrying out these commissions, man has by science discovered and utilized the laws which God had implanted in the world when he made it. Our quest for this kind of knowledge has yielded many practical results. We are the Wise Men of the West. Like Archimedes, we may not be able to move the earth, but only for lack of a fulcrum. We have made many changes. Like Columbus, we venture forth towards the unknown, only now the uncharted shores lie out there beyond the stars. Instead of our forward thrust slackening, there is every indication that it will quicken.

It would be interesting to know what "image" our age will enjoy after fifty or a hundred years. As our wisdom literature is largely that of mathematicians, astronomers, engineers, and physicists, succeeding generations may look upon us as quite one-sided and limited creatures; there is much more to life than science. Salvation does not depend on computers, math, or physics; a man can save his soul without knowing the ins and outs of this world at all. Wise

St. Augustine once remarked that "God does not ask us to become mathematicians, but saints." One can almost hear the reader's sigh of relief!

The second kind of knowledge-wisdom is one which revolves about revelation. One has to examine revelation no less diligently and carefully than he does the stars or the atom. Theology does not use electronic microscopes, but reason illumined by faith. The green fields of theology are also beckoning to intelligent laymen of the stature of Sheed, DeKonnick, Maritain, and others. From such men the Church has every right to expect deeper insights into the unfathomable riches of God. In the Church, as in life, one hand washes the other; the good one man does will be of profit to many.

The third and last kind of knowledge cannot be acquired by human effort, but is attained only by divine gift. It is that swift, subtle, unerring gift of wisdom, whereby a man, docile to the promptings of the Holy Spirit, is instantly led to judge as he should concerning the present, existential moment.

Have we then shown you the face of Wisdom? More than knowledge, it is the precious ability to judge rightly in matters relating to life and conduct. It manifests itself in soundness of judgment in the matter of means and ends. Yet wisdom is more than an ability to absorb truth or to master the art of applying this knowledge to desired ends. It chooses the right means to attain its ends, reshapes and inserts knowledge into human living. Wisdom, in other words, cuts across all specialties and technologies, orienting what is true in them to human understanding, human needs, and human hope. It is wisdom that brings the sciences and the humanities together in one magnificent universe of discourse not only with man and nature but also with God.

DOMINIC AND WISDOM

It may safely be assumed that St. Dominic did not know much about the natural sciences; in those days, few people did, and what they knew was elementary. The hour of natural science had not yet struck. But Dominic was outstanding in the other two departments of wisdom: He was a sound, clear-headed theologian, and at the same time sensitive and docile to the Holy Spirit. The order he established, still flourishing after more than eight centuries, proves his wisdom. When he dispersed the brethren two by two through-out Europe, they might have remonstrated with him that he was ruining the Order before it had even taken deep root. But his vision and judgment were clear and certain; he had rightly assessed the inner promptings of the Spirit. This was the proper means to attain his end, and God's. It was bread cast upon the waters (Eccles 11:1), something ventured, initiative, everything that God wanted of him. He made his great plans with wisdom.

How refreshing to see a saint like Dominic, a man marked by breadth of vision and by a total lack of narrow-mindedness. How heartening to see his calm acceptance and evaluation of facts, and his judicious, far-sighted adaptation of them, always keeping his goal in view. One does not picture him as a prisoner of the immediate present, although he lived in it; nor as a man harried and worried by a sea of complications and details. Decision, clarity, effectiveness attended him. Looking back, we can see that his solution was so perfect that it betrays something of the divine wisdom that inspired it. Dominic was a wise, wise man.

THE ATTAINMENT OF WISDOM

How does one go about becoming wise? Anything so precious as wisdom must surely have a high price attached to it. A sharing of one of God's most notable attributes, precious wisdom is usually given only to those who are willing to work for it. Good scientists or good theologians never count the cost of their wisdom. More often than not, their quest for it resembles Jacob's long servitude for the hand of Rachel (Gen 29:1ff.). They are like Jacob in this, that their love for wisdom more than matches his love for Rachel—and that was so grteat that the long years under Laban seemed to him as but a single day. The task itself is filled and fills with joy.

Age alone does not bring wisdom, although wisdom is perhaps oftenest found in those who are advanced in years. Acquired wisdom does not result from committee meetings, from shared activities, from any one single effort. Wisdom comes only after constant application and keeping the doors of the mind open to God and to all creation.

Such arduous preparation is normally the necessary prelude to wisdom. Such however is divine generosity that wisdom is given as a gift in baptism, or upon entry into the state of grace. Everyone has wisdom enough, therefore, to save his soul.

DOMINIC AND WATER

Dominic's sons and daughters should be, like him, wise. But if they are not fountains or wells of wisdom but only little receptacles, thimbles even, their wisdom will be limited and insignificant. Yet, St. Dominic would doubtless say that God requires no one to be greater than he was made. One has only to tip his own thimble, sharing his wisdom, leaving the rest to God. Floods of living water inundating the earth may, if God so please, flow from even a tiny source:

> I went forth like a canal from a river and like a water channel into a garden. I said, "I will water my orchard and drench my garden plot"; and lo, my canal became a river, and my river became a sea. I will again make instruction shine forth like the dawn, and I will make it shine afar; I will again pour out teaching like prophecy, and leave it to all future generations. Observe that I have not labored for myself alone, but for all who seek instruction. (Sir 24:30–34.)

St. Dominic, wise man that you are, dispense unto us the precious waters of your wisdom, so necessary to keep the gardens of our faith and good works green and flourishing, to God's greater honor and glory. And help us to be ever-flowing fountains of wisdom, as befits apostles.

Blessed are those who hunger
and thirst for justice

Dominic Converts the Innkeeper

6

Preacher of Grace

Our day is not, it would seem, a day of great preachers, nor one notable for great sermons. On the ecclesiastical horizon today there are few John Chrysostoms, few Lacordaires, few Tom Burkes, or Charles McKennas, and not many Fulton Sheens. Yet our ears do not go unfilled. Two industries undreamed-of a few short decades ago have captured much of the brains, imagination, skills, and eloquence of our day, and from media torrents of artful persuasion pour forth daily into the eyes and ears of listeners and viewers. "Buy this, buy that." The modern world has indeed its great orators, but they are for the most part in advertising and sales.

Can it be that God has so little to be said for him that he has no great orators to plead his cause before a modern world? Perish the thought. God always has heralds. But we must recognize the fact that what God once deigned to use had frequently been replaced by something as good, and sometimes even better. It is doubtful that the great preachers of old would, if they spoke to a modern audience, still command the attention and respect they did in their own day. But in any case, God is not the victim of his creation, time. When the right moment arrives, he raises up the right preacher. In the thirteenth century, that preacher's name was Dominic, and we salute him still as the *Preacher of Grace*.

PREACHER

St. Dominic was a much traveled and a tireless preacher. His great zeal to make God known led him to preach even to strangers. Once, for example, he encountered a group of German pilgrims, and proceeded to speak to them about God. Nor did God fail his spokesman, and Dominic was given the gift of tongues so that they might understand what he was saying.

Preaching, in St. Dominic's day, was called "Holy Preaching," or the "Preaching of Jesus Christ." It was not just a tool of defense, but the means he selected as the hallmark of his order. The Dominicans were to be like their founder, evangelical, gospel-minded men, fitted out to sow the good news to all men.

The word *gospel* means "good news" or glad tidings. For most of us, good news means a raise in pay, a new car, a new washing machine, or a lowering of taxes. Good news! We have just launched another spacecraft successfully. Good news! I have tickets to the game, or to the play. Good news! My mother is coming for a visit! Good news! I got a promotion!

But surely this is not the best we can do for good news. The gospel story is not something old, but is perennially fresh, new, exciting. The news that God himself came down upon earth in Christ Jesus is not any old news item of momentary interest. The Incarnation is a stupendous, unheard-of event, one carefully prepared for. The story of that preparation goes back in the Old Testament as far as with Adam and Eve. Despite the fact that man has always shown himself to be a resister of God, God never abandoned his fickle creature, man. It was God who initiated a covenant with a people he freely chose to be his own people, and that covenant, sealed on Mt. Sinai, was but a preparation for that remarkable covenant between God and man which was established by the Incarnation.

The great theme of the great orators of the ages has always been that of the good news of salvation through Jesus Christ, the Son of God. What manner of man is worthy to announce such news? The answer to this question is found in the New Testament.

"I have been chosen by God," St. Paul writes, "to be *a herald* of Jesus Christ." A preacher, then, no matter what name he bears, is one who proclaims the glad message of salvation through Christ. Dominic, an apostle cast in the mold of the great St. Paul, was like him a man who had been sent, an evangelical man, bringing to sinners the message of the gospel. St. Paul refers to himself as *the servant of Christ*. This word summons to memory the famous *Servant of*

Yahweh,[1] who is described as God's *polished arrow* (Is 49:2). A polished arrow is one upon which the arrowsmith has lavished careful attention, so that the arrow could be trusted to go where it was directed. Apply this to a preacher: God sends his preachers as an archer directs his arrows, straight to the target. The preacher is also called a *deacon*, or God's helper. God of course does not need any help from anybody, but it is his way to give those to whom he has given certain abilities, ample opportunity to use them. How kind of God not to do everything by himself, but to share his causality with man! The preacher is sometimes styled an *underling*, or *minister*, a term descriptive of the slave who manned an oar in a warship. It was not the galley slave's business to direct the ship—the helmsman could be relied on to do that—but to keep the ship moving. The preacher must then be a voice, even if he sometimes finds himself crying out his message in a wilderness. God has directed him there. Another description of a preacher or evangelical man is, *steward*. One who had the gospel mysteries entrusted to him for safekeeping and for increasing has a heavy responsibility on his shoulders. A steward must dispense his master's goods as needful, but at the same time must be prepared to defend what has been committed to his care. Crowning all these terms, and the key to the paradox of a preacher, a man who announces divine things, is the great title, *God's fellow worker*. Every preacher works with God, and for him.

---

1.   The Servant Songs are found in Is 42:1–4; 49:1–6; 50:4–11; 52:13–53:12.

Grace

Once when the apostles were gathered about Jesus, Philip asked him, "Master, show us the Father, and that is enough for us" (Jn 14:8). Jesus patiently replied, "Have I been with you for so long a time and you still do not know me, Philip? Whoever has seen me has seen the Father" (Jn 14:9). In fact, Jesus is the perfect image of the invisible God. In a more modern idiom we might say that Christ is the sacrament and sign of man's encounter with God. He is a sacred and sensible sign of God's infinite love and redeeming mercy. He is God's Word.

St. Dominic was not a writing man and we have none of his works other than a letter or two. His contemporaries, however, agreed that he was constantly preaching about God, or communing with him. It requires no stretch of the imagination to conclude that his preaching centered about Christ and his mother. How could he not have been impressed by the graciousness of God, who "while we were still sinners Christ died for us." (Rom 5:8). St. John explicitly says, "In this way the love of God was revealed to us: God sent his only Son into the world so that we might have life through him" (1 Jn 4:9). Other snatches of the gospel include, "God sent the spirit of his Son into our hearts, crying out, 'Abba, Father!'" (Gal 4:6) and "Now this is everlasting life, that they may know you, the only true God, and him whom you have sent, Jesus Christ" (Jn 17:3). The apostolic heart of Dominic overflowed with such good news, with the wonderful message of salvation, of eternal life begun by a sharing in God's own life here on earth. Truly does he merit the title of *Preacher of Grace.*

Some dispute Dominic's connection with the Rosary, but none can contest his devotion to Christ and the Passion. Fra Angelico has depicted the three great Dominican saints: Dominic, Thomas Aquinas, and Catherine, at the foot of the Cross. It is interesting and instructive to see these spiritual giants, the father and two of his greatest children, thus contemplating the climax of Jesus' life on earth. It is indeed the climax, for it was at this moment that Christ was redeeming the human race. In a few short hours the Father would signify his acceptance of that perfect sacrifice by raising his Son from the dead. "Jesus our Lord, who was put to death for our trespasses," St. Paul notes, "and raised for our justification" (Rom 4:25).

Jesus' whole life was a good example of man's perfect response to God. Christ now is invisible, seated at God's right hand in glory. When he returns on Judgment Day, he will usher in the final stage of the universe. Meanwhile, we keep history alive and relevant to our day not only by memory and faith, but in the sacrament. Man encounters him anew in the sacraments, which are God's gracious loving gestures towards those who live centuries after the saving event itself.

We remarked at the beginning the dearth of great preachers in our day, and made the point that God should not therefore be adjudged weak or helpless. His arms are not shortened; he simply has different plans from one age to another. He has a different, a new and exciting plan, for our day.

AGE OF THE LAITY

It ought to be quite obvious, judging from Vatican Council II and the present *aggiornamento*, that God is still preaching in the world. But now he preaches in a different way. The good news is now sent forth in a truly novel way with a clarion call unheard before. For now, it seems clear, God wants his preaching done not so much by the man in the pulpit, but by everyone who is united to Christ in faith and in charity. It is the *age of the laity*, and of the individual Christian who proclaimed in words, namely that the world and all things in it are good and must be sanctified and used for God's honor and glory. Man's destiny is, in a word, nothing short of God himself. It is a destiny which man can realize with the help of God's grace. Good news!

God's layman also fits the gospel picture of the preacher. He is a herald, proclaiming by his behavior and faithfulness to his religious duties the fact that God has come down upon earth and covenanted with man. The layman is to be a lay apostle, one sent to deliver the message of tremendous import—God is interested in man. This deserves to be proclaimed from the housetops. The layman is God's servant, slave, special instrument, witness, steward, dispenser of divine mysteries. He is, in a word, God's co-worker.

The preachers of old occupied (as good talkers usually do) the center of the stage. They were much in the public eye. Today, however, God's ministers are generally those who preach by their lives and example. They are the only book some people ever read, the only voice some ever hear raised in praise and defense of God. Their lives are *hidden*, as St. Paul assured the Colossians, with Christ in God (cf. Col 3:3).

Our lives then should be a preaching, an expression of our sacramental being, and visible signs of God's invisible grace. Grace is made visible through personal holiness. And that is a worthy mission for Dominic's sons and daughters who, in any way God wishes, preach the good news of God's love for man.

Death and Glorification of Saint Dominic

7

Join Us to the Blessed

Fame, often unflatteringly compared to a woman, is curiously unpredictable. No one would ever have imagined that it should have descended upon the abodes of the dead, yet it has done so, not once but often. Paris can boast its famous cemetery *Père Lachaise*, in which the hapless Abelard and beautiful Heloise lie buried side by side. Genoa's *Cimitero di Staglieno*, a forest of ambitious and highly imaginative funerary monuments, is a deserving tourist attraction. Here one can see and marvel at deathbed scenes, the Angel of Judgment, the resurrection of the dead, life-size statues of the occupants of the tombs, and even ships, symbolically arrested at full sail. But America has its unusual cemeteries too. In New Orleans the dead are buried above ground because of the water level; while in New York there is a Jewish cemetery where space problems make it necessary to bury people in a standing position. Along the bluffs which overlook the Mississippi, mysterious Indian mounds, some bear-shaped, others in the form of flying birds, all of them pointing downstream, extend for miles southwards. It gives one to think.

We are going to talk about death and what happens after death because St. Dominic is saluted as one who can help us get to heaven.

DEATH

Death is a part of human existence. At birth it can be said of everyone, "This child is dying. He shall not recover." Again, "it is appointed that human beings die once, and after this the judgment" (Heb 9:27). History provides many examples (amusing, were they not so pitiful) of man's efforts to evade death. Many today also find it more acceptable to say that their friends have passed away, or are at rest, than to use even the word *death*. Perhaps it is because we are awed by the silence of the grave, by the completely personal aspect of death. It is so absolutely final, and spells separation from what we call life and time. The life from which man departs is mysterious in itself; death ushers in a totally new kind of existence. The mystery is too much for us to cope with. It unsettles us and we don't even like to talk about it.

The ancient peoples of the Near East believed that the afterlife was to be a continuation of their present existence: kings would continue on as kings, and slaves as slaves. Only in Israel did there emerge, under the guidance of the Holy Spirit, a better notion of what was to come. At first the Israelites thought that after death, all descended into a place underneath the earth, called Sheol. Happiness seems not to have been associated with it, for the dead there led a dark, shadowy kind of existence; apparently it was not a place for prayers even (Ps 28:1; 30:8 f.). Along with this, the Jews of old firmly believed that God rewarded the good in this life by granting them wealth, length of days, many children, good crops, good health, and so on. But the Hebrews were too realistic not to notice that life seldom ran according to this scheme; the good did suffer (witness the case of Job), and the wicked frequently had the best of this life. Eventually however the picture cleared, and it was seen that in the afterlife the good will be rewarded for the good they had done on earth and consoled for the trials they had there endured. As for the wicked, they would receive their just deserts in the next life (Wis 3:1–19). Heaven awaited the good, hell the wicked.

HEAVEN

Most people, it must be confessed, find it difficult to work up much enthusiasm about heaven. They think of it mostly in terms of going to church on Sunday, which for them pretty generally means Dullsville. Who wants to go to church forever and ever? Who gets excited over the prospect of a perpetual hymn singing? Even if the musical accompaniment were to be that of heavenly harps! Singing hymns and/or sitting on clouds forever would be a dismal way to spend eternity, and anyone with intelligence would find that woefully inadequate.

Heaven of course is not like that at all. The music that bubbles up in heaven from the lips of the blessed is the music of sheer delight. It is caused by the sight of God.

But can eternal happiness come from something that is seen? Life as we know it gives us some clue to the answer here. It is enough to make us happy here on earth when a beloved one rejoins us, when a dear friend walks into a room. "Let me look at you," is often on our lips, as if the very sight of a loved one were in itself a cause for greater joy. On earth we hungrily seek out the good, the true, and the beautiful, and we are forever dissatisfied with what we find. A reflection of God's goodness is simply not enough.

> The Master is so fair
> So sweet his smile to fallen men,
> That those who see him unaware,
> Can never rest in peace again.

In heaven, however, one no longer has to bother with half-glimpses or finite beauty. God is the *summum bonum*, all good, recapitulating in himself the fragmentary goodness and beauty and truth which so fleetingly captivate and disappoint us during our mortal life. But God far exceeds our greatest expectations; the very sight of him spells supreme and unalloyed happiness.

Centuries ago, in the imperfect revelation of the Old Testament, it was said, "No man shall see God and live." But these were not God's last words on the subject. The New Testament tells us that after death the souls of the just will, thanks to a gift of the light of glory, be able to gaze upon God. "At present we see indistinctly, as in a mirror, but then face to face. At present I know partially; then I shall know fully, as I am fully known" (1 Cor 13:12) and "Night will be no more, nor will they need light from lamp or sun, for the Lord God shall give them light, and they shall reign forever and ever" (Rev 22:5).

Sight is the most spiritual of our senses, and it is not at first glance evident how seeing and happiness go hand in hand. Yet almost everyone has, at some time or other, experienced the excitement and exhilaration that attends an interesting lecture, or a lively discussion. In such encounters time flies by on winged feet. Intellectually one is deeply involved; high demands are made upon his mental resources. A man forgets the clock when his mind is working furiously at top capacity. And it is at such moments that he is at his best, when he is most himself, most human—thinking, reasoning, contemplating, and loving the truth.

In heaven, such thrilling experiences will be multiplied by infinity. Heaven is not an eternal vacation in which there is nothing to do; it is a place of intense activity of mind and will. If on earth we derive pleasure from trifling bits of knowledge, what will it not be like when, in the beatific vision, we shall see the maker of all things, the Lord of heaven and earth?

The implications of "seeing God" are many and great. The blessed shall gaze upon God for all eternity without ever being able to say that they "know it all." Heaven is an unending, dizzying, thrilling, endless voyage of discovery of the unfathomable depths of God. In seeing God, the blessed shall see everything they failed to see while on earth. Heavenly knowledge is not limited to the few city blocks which made up their neighborhood, nor to a few miles of town or city, nor to a few years of life. In God, waiting to be enjoyed by the blessed, are all the perfections of all creation. The wonders of the universe, the mysteries of space, the hidden things of the earth and ocean, all will be there as in an open book.

Naturally, our thoughts turn to our relatives, friends, and acquaintances. What about them? The answer is always the same: In God the blessed see and know all that they need to make them perfectly happy. In the beatific vision each man and woman will be able to read the full story of all the thoughts, hopes, and struggles of parents and friends, of loved ones still on earth, of the souls in purgatory, and even of the angels and the other blessed. Stated in other terms this means that in heaven we shall know our own. Husbands will as never before know their wives, parents their children, friends their friends. This reunion in God will not be marred with sobs, tearful embraces, protestations of love; all will together share God, and rejoice in sharing the blessed vision with their dear ones.

We implore St. Dominic to "join us with the blessed in heaven." This audacious request must be properly understood, and the matter is sufficiently important to warrant a few words about the Communion of Saints.

COMMUNION OF SAINTS

This doctrine is explicitly stated in the Apostles' Creed. It means that there is a fellowship existing between all who love God. It implies that the living and the dead, whether human or angelic, are interested in each other, and intercede for one another in prayer and deed.

Now of course we should not imagine that this doctrine implies a rivalry between the saints and God, as if they can sometimes do something he cannot. Prayer to the saints does not suggest that God must occasionally take a back seat, or that the saints know something about people on earth that he does not. Rather, it is God who allows the saints in heaven to know of the prayers directed to them from men. Why should he do this? Because by their great efforts for his kingdom and for men during their lifetime on earth, the saints as it were earned the right to be listened to after their death. In heaven they are no longer in a position to earn or merit anything (they left all that behind when they entered into eternal life) and are moreover in actual possession of their reward. But it is still possible for them to appeal to God that he grant, out of his infinite liberality, what neither they, nor their petitioners on earth, deserve in justice. Is it illogical to suppose that God will not lend a willing ear to the prayers of the saints in our behalf? It seems, in fact, that he favors certain saints. At any rate, prayers to St. Ann have often produced a husband, those to St. Anthony have led to the recovery of lost articles, and so on. The explanation of this might lie in God's intention to draw attention to this or that saint.

HEAVENLY INTERCESSOR

By his penitential and apostolic life, St. Dominic earned the right to be listened to in heaven. That he would be interested in his children, and in those who prayed to him, is gracefully recalled in the *O Spem Miram*, a second antiphon composed in his honor by Constantine de Medici. It is worth our attention:

> O wonderful hope which you [Dominic] gave to those mourning for you at the hour of death! You promised that after death you would help your brethren. Fulfill, O Father, your promise, assisting us by your prayers. Do you, who were outstanding for many miracles wrought in the bodies of the sick, heal our sick souls, and bring to us the aid of Christ.

The importance of living with an eye on the next life is too obvious to need restating. St. Paul reminded his friends of this when he wrote, "Our citizenship [or commonwealth] is in heaven (Philemon 3:20). What he meant can be easily explained. In the days when England had her colonies, English public servants far from home were careful to dress punctiliously for dinner and to observe at that meal all the customs and formalities to which they had been accustomed at home. This was to remind them that they were not uncivilized and uncultured, as their charges in undeveloped Africa and India often were, but rather, members of a great nation. The practice kept them from "going native" or "going to seed."

Those who are called to be citizens of heaven, that is, all those who have been baptized and received the sacraments, must therefore keep before their eyes the goal toward which they are moving. If they become enmeshed in this life, chances are they will forget what manner of men they are.

Prayer to St. Dominic keeps us mindful of the fact that we exiles are burdened with our sins, and need his help both in order to live in this world, and to increase in the love of God. By his powerful intercession, those who endeavor to follow in his footsteps may hopefully look forward to that blessed vision which constitutes eternal life. "What no eye has seen, nor ear heard, nor the heart of man conceived, what God has prepared for those who love him" (1 Cor 2:9).[1]

---

1.   The reader is invited to consult the profound and detailed words on St. Dominic, *Saint Dominic, His Times and His Works* by M. H. Vicaire, O.P. (New York: McGraw-Hill, 1964), and *The History of the Dominican Order* by William A. Hinnebusch, O.P. (Staten Island: Alba House, 1966).

Made in the USA
San Bernardino, CA
12 October 2016